C000285268

The Way of Humility

by
Jorge Cardinal Bergoglio
(Pope Francis)

*All booklets are published thanks to the
generous support of the members of the
Catholic Truth Society*

CATHOLIC TRUTH SOCIETY
PUBLISHERS TO THE HOLY SEE

Contents

All rights reserved. This edition first published 2013 by The Incorporated Catholic Truth Society, 40-46 Harleyford Road London SE11 5AY Tel: 020 7640 0042 Fax: 020 7640 0046. Copyright © 2013 The Incorporated Catholic Truth Society in this English language edition. Translated from the original Spanish Edition by Helena Scott. Original Spanish edition **Sobre la acusación de si mismo** *published by Editorial Claretiana, Casa Central Lima 1360, 1138 Buenos Aires, Argentina © 2005 Editorial Claretiana (Misioneros Claretianos Provincia San José del Sur).*

ISBN 978 1 86082 874 4

Preface

On beginning the path of the Archdiocesan Assembly, I asked that we would place ourselves in a spirit of prayer, that we would pray very much for the Assembly, and that we would offer, with a penitential attitude, some sacrifice to our Lord, some mortification to accompany our prayer during this time. I suggested that this sacrifice might be that of not speaking badly of each other. As I am aware that we find it difficult, I think it is a good thing to offer up. The spirit of the unity of the Church is harmed by back-biting and criticism. St Augustine described it as follows: "There are men who judge rashly, who slander, whisper and murmur, who are eager to suspect what they do not see, and eager to spread abroad things they do not even suspect" (Sermon 47, 12). Negative criticism leads us to focus on the faults and failings of other people; like that, we can feel superior. The prayer of the publican in the Temple (*Lk* 18:11-12) illustrates this, and Jesus warned us against looking for the speck in someone else's eye and ignoring the plank in our own.

Speaking badly of others is harmful for the whole Church, because it doesn't stop there: it moves on to become aggression (at least in our hearts). St Augustine calls backbiters "men without remedy". "Men without remedy are those who cease to concentrate on their own sins in order to focus on other people's. They do not look for something to correct, but something they can criticise. And, being themselves without excuse, they are always ready to accuse other people" (Sermon 19). And, he says, "The only thing that remains to them is the sickness of animosity, and the more they think this makes them strong, the weaker they are rendered by their sickness" (Commentary on Psalm 32, 29). To guard against this bad spirit (of speaking badly of others), Christian tradition, from the first Desert Fathers onwards, proposes the practice of self-accusation.

Many years ago I wrote an article on the subject of self-accusation. Although it was addressed to young religious, I think it may be good for all of us. I offer it as a contribution to this Assembly. The article was inspired by some of the writings of St Dorotheus of Gaza, which are added at the end to complete it.

May our Lord help us to progress in the Archdiocesan Assembly in a spirit of prayer, offering the sacrifice of not speaking badly of one another.

Jorge Mario Cardinal Bergoglio, SJ
Buenos Aires, 16th July 2005,
Feast of Our Lady of Mount Carmel

Self-Accusation[1]

Introduction

The reflections of St Dorotheus of Gaza provide us with an opportunity to raise the problem of self-accusation and its effect on the spiritual life, and especially the effect it has on the union of hearts within a community.

It is not rare to find in communities, whether at the local or the provincial level, groups that aim to impose their own thinking and preferences on everyone else. This tends to happen when loving openness to one's neighbour is replaced by attachment to one's own ideas. Then we don't defend the family as a whole, but just "my part" of it. We don't give our allegiance to the unity that shapes and builds up the body of Christ, but to conflict that divides, separates and weakens. And for formators and superiors, it is not always easy to form in people a sense of belonging to a family spirit, especially when it is a question of forming inner attitudes that are small in themselves, but that have a repercussion at the level of the institution, of the body as a whole.

One of the solid attitudes that need to be formed in the heart of young religious is that of *self-accusation*, because an absence of self-accusation is what causes partisanship and divisions.

Throughout this essay I will be quoting various passages from the works of St Dorotheus of Gaza, preceded by a short consideration of the effects of an attitude of self-accusation.

Self-accusation is an act of courage

And in the first place we need to discard any element of the hypocritical idea that self-accusation is childish, cowardly or somehow neurotic.

On the contrary, self-accusation requires uncommon courage in order to open the door to the discovery of things we did not know about ourselves and let other people see beyond our façade. It means doing away with cosmetics, so that the truth can be plainly shown.

At the basis of self-accusation (which is a means to an end), lies a fundamental choice against individualism, a choice instead of the family spirit of the Church that leads us to behave as good sons and daughters, good brothers and sisters, so as to become, in due course, good parents. Self-accusation implies a fundamentally community outlook.

The dangers of individualism

When individualism grows, it leads to partisanship within community life. The temptation to individualism starts off from a truth (which may be real, or partly real, or only apparent, or a complete fallacy[2]). It is generally a "reason" that both justifies and soothes us. And that "reason" is rooted in the spirit of and suspiciousness and supposition.

Suppositions are like daydreams: they are always a temptation. God is not in them, because he is the Lord of real time, the measurable past and the actual present. As for the future, he is the Lord of the Promise who asks us for trust and abandonment.

The spirit of suspicion and supposition aims basically for a truth that asserts me against my brother. It is always a truth that defends me against community participation, that justifies me for not taking part with the community.

In the teaching of Dorotheus of Gaza it is the devil himself who sows suspicion in people's hearts in order to divide them from one another. This phenomenon works in the opposite direction to the Incarnation of the Word: the devil aims to *divide* (through means of suspicion) in order to *confuse* afterwards. Our Lord, by contrast, is always God and Man, *indivise et inconfuse* - without division of person, without confusion of natures.

When the devil sows suspicion he tries to convince us by means of lies (cf. *Spiritual Exercises* 315, Second Rule for the First Week, and 332, Fourth Rule for the Second Week), or half-truths, to manipulate our hearts into selfish convictions that lead us into a world closed off from all objectivity (cf. *Spiritual Exercises* 326, Thirteenth Rule for the First Week to discern spirits).

Suspicion, sown by the devil, sets up a crooked measuring-rod in the heart, which displaces and twists everything. It is not easy to straighten out a religious who is tempted by the possession of a crooked measure of this kind. It is no longer a question of sorting out this or that wrong idea, but a whole hermeneutic - the way they interpret everything. Everything that happens is interpreted in a twisted way, because the measure they apply to it is itself crooked.

In this *Boletín de Espiritualidad*, I have sometimes referred to the phrase "They had no right to do this to me", used by discontented nuns, which St Teresa of Avila said[3] does so much harm in religious life.

Religious who are tempted in this way end up being "collectors of injustices". They spend their lives keeping a careful list of all the injuries that others have done them, or that they think others have done them. This frequently leads to a "conspiracy theory victim" spirituality.

In sociology, the conspiracy theory, from the hermeneutical point of view, is the weakest type of hermeneutic there is. It cannot stand up to serious reasoning. It is an elementary cause of someone being led astray, occurring in the type of person who basically longs for a simplistic goodies-versus-baddies set-up (and they count themselves among the goodies). Becoming disconnected from objective reality, they wall themselves up in a sort of defensive ideology. They swap doctrine for ideology, and exchange the patient pilgrimage of God's children for the complex of being victims of a conspiracy set up against them by others - the baddies, their superiors, the other members of their community. They end up trapped in a web of words, and this accords with what Tomáš Špidlík said: that words born of the mind are a wall, while words born of the heart are a bridge.

We can say that these men's minds are sick. And when we confuse the mind with intellectual capacity, we forget that the mind was damaged by original sin. As Daniélou said, how many people there are who take pride in their intellectual capacity, and forget that their minds are deeply wounded, sick, and destructive (because a damaged mind also damages the minds of those around it). But let's not forget that a mind is sick and continues to be sick because of a passion that "imprisons the truth" (cf. *Rm* 1:18 ff.).

Anxiety: the loss of peace

Alongside that attitude, there grows a "state of anxiety" that is also a bad spirit.

Having fallen into the habit of being suspicious about everything, such people little by little lose the peace of mind that comes from trusting confidence in God. The right way towards conflict resolution, they imagine, must always pass through the filter of their constant control. They are continually shaken by anxiety, the result of their combination of anger and laziness.

They follow Herod, who was "perturbed" (cf. *Mt* 2:3), and the High Priests and the Pharisees, who in their agitation tried to put a limit to the power of God by sealing up a tomb (cf. *Mt* 27:62-66). They want to find a solution to all their fears in the illusion of their own omnipotent control, and they know nothing of God's sweetness, which renders the power of his enemies merely relative, reducing them to smouldering stumps:

> Then the heart of the king and the hearts of the people shuddered as the trees of the forest shudder in front of the wind. The Lord said… "'Pay attention, keep calm, have no fear, do not let your heart sink because of these two smouldering stumps of firebrands.'" (*Is* 7:2-4)

A hidden self-indulgence

This mechanism of suspicion, cloaked in love for the truth, hides a particular kind of self-indulgence. Behind all their ideas they are trying to conceal their self-will. Such religious are habitually over-critical, and with their storm of arguments, all that they really prove is their adherence to hidden self-gratification.

Suspicion and suspiciousness lead men to the classic bitterness of those who are ready to accuse God. Dorotheus of Gaza highlights this in the case of Adam and Eve. And little by little such religious turn away from the truth and become entangled in lies. There is also, at the bottom of this enlisting on the side of lies, a displacement of the capacity for condemnation. They are unable to condemn rightly. They confuse battle with noise and clamour. They have not, as St Ignatius teaches in the Triple Colloquium of the Third Exercise of the First Week, prayed for the grace to "know in order to hate" (*Spiritual Exercises* 62-63). Curiously, they are usually ethicists, who counterbalance the guilt produced in them by their suspicion of everyone, with an affected pretence of not condemning anyone or anything. Because they lack all sense of objectivity, their imaginations condemn *a priori* as suspect all attempts by others to come close to them in their personal lives.

Self-accusation: a pre-emption and remedy

The spiritual teaching of self-accusation or self-contempt, expounded by St Dorotheus of Gaza, aims to nip all such temptations in the bud, and, echoing the tradition he received from the Fathers of the Church, to place the religious within the objective truth of his relations to God and other people. The constant exercise of self-accusation forestalls all suspicion, and leaves room for the action of God, who is the one who ultimately brings about the union of hearts.

By self-accusation the heart of the religious abases itself, and it is precisely that inner self-abasement that enables all other natural and artificial means of mutual understanding to be effective.

This attitude of abasement has a theological foundation in the self-abasement (*synkatábasis*, literally "condescension") of the Word, which is what makes our access to God possible (see the theology of the *Letter to the Hebrews*: 2:17; 3:7ff.; 4:14-16; and 9). Therefore it is

Christ himself who gives us access to our brother, starting off from our own self-abasement.

This is the really Christian way of getting close to someone. Getting close to someone has a qualitative element that lifts all religious closeness (filial, fraternal and paternal) into the eschatological sphere that makes it a reality once and for all.

Additionally, it is our Lord himself who justifies this self-abasement on our part. The Pharisees justified themselves ("you look to one another for approval" *Jn* 5:44). The just man only seeks justification from God, and therefore he abases himself, and accuses himself. And just as justification was given to us by Christ's cross, in a universal and unrepeatable way, our walking along the path of our Lord means that we too must take up the self-abasement of the cross. Self-accusation means accepting the role of the guilty person, as our Lord accepted it, and was burdened with our guilt. Man feels guilty, deserving of punishment. Hence, St Ignatius takes care to recommend "humiliating and abasing oneself" to whoever is receiving consolation (cf. Eleventh Rule on the discernment of spirits, *Spiritual Exercises* 324) in case the pursuit of consolations should lead them to set themselves up as having merits that they do not really possess.

Humiliation and humility

Self-accusation is always an act of humiliation which leads to humility. And when one opts for the path of humiliation, one is necessarily opting for fighting and victory.

As Maximus the Confessor said, the *synkatábasis* of the Word is a lure for the devil, who swallows the bait and dies. "Thus he offers his flesh as a bait to the insatiable hunger of hell's dragon, arousing its greed; and the bait, once swallowed, becomes mortal poison and, because of the power of the divinity within it, causes the dragon's total downfall; that same power would serve, by contrast, as a remedy for human nature, restoring it to its original dignity" (*Centuries* 1, 12). Humiliating oneself means somehow attracting the devil's attention, fighting, subjecting oneself to temptation, but in the end, winning.

This attitude, unlike the suspiciousness that produces anxiety, leads to meekness and patience. The rules of modesty written by St Ignatius are based on a paragraph in the *Constitutions* that describe this state of meekness:

Let all take special care to guard the doors of their senses very diligently, especially their eyes and ears and tongue, from all disorder; and to keep their soul in peace and true humility, shown in silence when silence should be kept, and, when it is necessary to speak, in considerate and edifying speech, and in the modesty of their faces and the maturity of their gait and all their movements, free from all sign of impatience or pride; trying and desiring to give place to others, valuing all others from the heart as superior to themselves, and outwardly showing them the respect and reverence due to each person's position, with mildness and religious simplicity; so that by consideration for one another they may grow in devotion, and praise God our Lord, whom each should try to recognise in the other, as in his image (*Constitutions* 250).

This text recalls Chapter 12 of the *Letter to the Romans*, and many other Pauline passages that speak of the "fruits of the Spirit". And it is precisely along this path of self-accusation that we reach the further conviction that St Ignatius had of himself: that he was "nothing but an obstacle".

Christian meekness is built up like that; it goes beyond the sphere of the rules of good manners, to attain its deepest root and its perfect model in the meekness of the Lamb.

Someone who accuses himself makes room for God's mercy to enter. He is like the publican who does not dare to raise his eyes (cf. *Lk* 18:13). Someone who accuses himself is a man who will always come close to others, like the good Samaritan, and in that way of coming close, Christ himself provides access to the other.

It may help us to understand all these things if we read slowly Chapters 2 and 3 of Book 2 of *The Imitation of Christ*, about humble submission and the good and peaceful man.

Dorotheus of Gaza on Self-Accusation

The numbers in the margins are those used in the Sources Chrétiennes edition: Dorothée de Gaza, *Oeuvres Spirituelles*, Du Cerf, Paris, 1963.

Instruction no. 7

79. We should consider, brethren, why it sometimes happens that something unpleasant is said to us, and we remain quite untroubled, as though we had not heard it; and at other times, we instantly get upset. What is the reason for the difference? There are, I believe, many reasons, but I think that one alone is at the root of all the others. Let me explain. For example, one brother has just finished his prayer or has made a good meditation, and so is "in good form". And he puts up with what his brother has said to him, and carries on with his affairs without minding it. Another is attached to his brother, and because of that liking, he peacefully accepts whatever comes to him from that brother. And it also happens that a brother despises the one who says the unpleasant thing, and considers whatever comes from that person as beneath contempt, not even rating him as a person, and taking no account of him or anything that he may say or do.

80. In the monastery, before I left it, there was a brother whom I never saw upset or annoyed at anyone. What is more, I saw that many of the brothers mistreated him and insulted him in different ways. This young monk bore with whatever anybody did to him as though nobody troubled him at all. I never ceased to admire his remarkable patience, and wondered how he had acquired such virtue. One day I called him apart and, making a deep reverence to him, asked him to tell me what thoughts he had in his heart, when he showed such patience amidst the insults and sufferings inflicted on him. He replied simply and frankly, "My custom is to see myself, with regard to those who do such things, just like a puppy with regard to its masters." At these words I bowed my head and said to myself, "This brother has found the way." I made the sign of the cross and left him, imploring God's protection on us both.

81. Sometimes the reason why we do not get upset is our contempt for our brother, and this is clearly disastrous. But when we do get upset with a brother who ill-treats us, our upset may originate in momentary bad dispositions, or in the dislike we feel for that brother. Very different reasons may also come into play. But if we carefully seek out the root cause of our upset, we always find the same: the fact that we do not practise self-accusation. This is why we feel crushed and never at peace. It is not surprising that all the saints say there is no other road than this. No one has found true peace by following any other road, and neither should we imagine

we will find it if we never consent to accuse ourselves. Indeed, even were we to perform a thousand good works, if we do not follow the road of self-accusation we will not fail to suffer ourselves and make others suffer, thus forfeiting all merit.

By contrast, what joy, what repose of spirit will be tasted wherever he goes by the man who accuses himself, as Abba Poemen says! He judges himself *a priori* to have deserved whatever injury, insult or suffering he may meet, and is never troubled or upset. What more carefree state could possibly exist?

82. But you may say: "If a brother is unpleasant to me, and on examining my conscience I find I have given him no cause, how can I accuse myself?" As a matter of fact, if anyone examines his conscience honestly and with the fear of God, he will certainly realise that he did give his brother cause, whether in word, action or attitude. And if he really should find that in none of these ways did he give his brother cause in the present case, it is nevertheless very probable that he was uncharitable towards that brother on some other occasion, or that he made another brother suffer, and for that very fault, or for another sin he committed, he does deserve this present ill-treatment. Therefore if we examine our behaviour in a God-fearing way and scrutinise our consciences carefully, we will always find that we are responsible in some way.

It also happens that a brother, believing himself to be in a state of peace and tranquillity, is angered by an unfriendly word addressed to him by someone, and considers that he is right to be angered, because he thinks: "If that person had not come and said that upsetting thing, I would not have sinned." That is an illusion, and faulty reasoning. Did the person who said the word put the brother's passion into it? No: but by that word he simply revealed the passion that was already within the brother, so that he might repent of it if he wished. This brother is like a wheaten loaf that is beautiful on the outside, but when it is cut open reveals that it is mouldy inside. He thought he was at peace, but there was a passion inside him that he did not know about or did not think important. A single word from his brother brought to light the mouldiness in his heart. If he wishes to obtain mercy, let him repent, let him purify himself, and in the end he will see that he ought to be grateful to his brother for having been the cause of this improvement.

83. If we follow this path, trials will not be so overwhelming, and the further we advance, the lighter they will appear. Indeed, as our souls grow, we become stronger and more capable of bearing everything that happens to us. It is like a beast of burden: if it is sturdy, it cheerfully carries the heavy burden that is loaded onto it. If it loses its balance it gets up straight away and suffers no harm. But if it is weak, any load is too much for it, and if it falls it needs a lot of help to get back on its feet.

The same is true of the soul. We are weakened every time we sin, because sin exhausts and corrupts the sinner. Anything at all is enough to overwhelm us then. But if, instead, we advance in virtue, what previously overcame us becomes more and more bearable. This is a great advantage to us, an abundant source of peace and progress, because it makes us ourselves responsible for what happens, not other people, especially since nothing can happen to us without God's providence.

84. But someone might say, "How can I avoid being tormented if I need something and don't receive it? In that case, I am compelled by my need." But even then there is no reason for accusing someone else, or being annoyed with someone. Someone who really believes they need something, if they do not get it, should say: "Christ knows better than I whether I should obtain satisfaction, and he himself will take care of this thing or this food." The children of Israel ate manna in the desert for forty years, and even though it was of a single kind, for each of them that manna became whatever he desired: savoury for the person who desired it to be savoury, sweet for the person who desired it to be sweet, adapting itself to the temperament of each of them (cf. *Ws* 16:21). If, then, someone needs to eat eggs and only receives vegetables, let him say, "If it had been useful for me to eat an egg, God would certainly have sent me one. On the other hand, it is possible that these

vegetables will be for me as though I were eating an egg."
I am sure that this will be counted by our Lord as though it
were martyrdom. Because if he is truly worthy to be heard,
God will incline the hearts even of the pagans in order to
show mercy to him according to his need. But if he is not
worthy, or if what he prays for is not useful for him, he
would find no satisfaction even if God made a new heaven
and a new earth. It is true that sometimes we receive more
than we need, and at other times less. Since God in his
mercy provides what is needful for each, if he gives more
than enough, it is to show us the excess of his tenderness,
and teach us to be grateful.

When, by contrast, God does not even give what we
need, he supplements with his word the thing that is
needed, and teaches us patience. Thus, in all things,
whether we receive good or evil, we should raise our eyes
and thank God for everything that happens, never failing to
accuse ourselves; and we should say with the Fathers, "If
something good comes to us, it is by God's disposition; if
evil comes to us, it is because of our sins."

Truly, all our sufferings come from our sins. The saints,
when they suffer, suffer for the sake of God's name, or
so that their virtue may be made manifest for the benefit
of many, or for an increase of the reward that will come
to them from God. But how could we say the same of
ourselves, poor wretches that we are? Daily do we sin,
and let ourselves be ruled by our passions; we have left

the straight path shown us by the Fathers, that consists of accusing ourselves; instead we follow the twisted path on which each accuses his neighbour. In all circumstances we are eager to blame our brother and impute faults to him. We live in carelessness, without concerning ourselves about anything, and yet we demand an account from our neighbour of how he is keeping the commandments.

85. Two quarrelling brothers came to see me one day. The older said of the younger: "When I give him an order, he gets annoyed, and so do I, because I think that if he had confidence and charity for me, he would willingly take in what I tell him." And the younger one said, "May Your Reverence forgive me: he certainly does not speak to me in a God-fearing way, but he wants to order me about, and that, I think, is why my heart has no confidence in him, according to the word of the Fathers."

We can see how these two brothers accused each other, and neither one accused himself.

Another two, who were each annoyed with the other, made deep reverences to each other but continued to feel angry. The first said, "He made me a reverence unwillingly, and that is why I have no confidence in him, according to the word of the Fathers." And the other said, "He was not charitably disposed towards me before I presented him with my excuses; therefore, I have no confidence in him either." Do you see the perversion of the human spirit? God knows how much it distresses me to see that we even use the words of the Fathers to serve our own bad will and ruin our souls. What was needful was for each of them to accuse himself. One should have said, "I made the reverence to my brother against my will; therefore our Lord did not inspire him with confidence towards me." And the other should have said, "I was not charitably disposed towards him before the reverence he did me; and for that reason, God did not give him confidence in me." It would have been necessary for the first two to have done the same. One ought to have said: "I speak out of self-regard, and therefore God does not give my brother confidence in me." And the other ought to have said: "My brother gives me orders with humility and charity, but I am not docile or God-fearing." Whereas in fact, neither of them was on the right path; neither of them accused himself. On the contrary, each of them accused his neighbour.

86. This is the reason why we do not manage to advance, or become even moderately useful. Instead we spend our time in corrupting ourselves by thinking badly of one another, and in tormenting ourselves. We each justify ourselves, we each neglect ourselves, as I have said, without noticing anything wrong; and instead, we prefer to demand an account from our neighbour of his observance of the commandments. And so we do not learn to do good; as soon as we receive a little light, immediately we call our neighbour to account, and accuse him, saying: "He ought

to do this; why did he do that?" But why do we not rather call ourselves to account over the commandments, and accuse ourselves of not keeping them?

Let us recall the holy old man who was once asked, "Father, which part of this way do you consider to be the greatest?" He answered, "Self-accusation in everything." His questioner praised him, and the holy old man added, "There is no other way than that."

In the same way, Abba Poemen groaned and said, "All the virtues have entered into this house except one, and without that one, it is difficult for a man to stay upright." He was asked which virtue it was, and he replied, "Self-accusation."

St Antony said that man's main task was to take responsibility for his own wrong-doing in God's sight, and to expect to be tempted until his last breath.

Everywhere, we find that the holy Fathers found peace of soul by observing this rule and referring everything, no matter how tiny, to God.

87. That was the reaction of a holy old man who was ill. His disciple put linseed oil, which is harmful, in his food instead of honey. The old man said nothing, and uncomplainingly ate a first and then a second portion, as was necessary, without accusing his brother or attributing his action to malice, and without saying a single word that might upset him. When the brother realised what he had done, he began to lament, saying, "I have given you death, Abba, and it was you who

made me commit this sin, by your silence." But the old man said gently, "Do not lament, my son. If God had wanted me to eat honey, it would have been honey that you gave me." In this way he referred the whole matter to God. But, good holy man, what did God have to do with all of this? Your brother committed an error, and you say "If God had wanted…" What is the connection? "Yes," said the old man. "If God had wanted me to eat honey, my brother would have given me honey." He was sick and had been unable to eat for many days; and yet he was not angered at his brother, but, referring the matter to God, he remained calm. The old man spoke wisely, since he knew that if God had wanted him to eat honey, he would have changed even that foul oil into honey.

88. As for us, brethren, how often we turn against our neighbour and shower him with reproaches, accusing him of contempt and of acting against his conscience! Do we hear a word? Instantly we take it badly and say, "If he had not wanted to wound me he would not have said that."

Think of the holy man who said, regarding Shimei, "Let him curse. If the Lord said to him, 'Curse David', what right has anyone to say, 'Why have you done this?'" (2 S 16:10). Did God order a murderer to curse the prophet? How could God have said this to him? But in his wisdom the prophet knew well that nothing attracts God's mercy upon the soul as much as trials, especially those that come in time of misfortune and persecution. He also said, "Let him curse on if the Lord has told him to." Why? "Perhaps the Lord will look on my misery and repay me with good for his curse today." See how wisely the prophet acted. He was angered at those who wished to punish Shimei for cursing him: "What business is it of mine and yours, sons of Zeruiah?" he said. "Let him curse on if the Lord has told him to."

How far we are from saying, with reference to our brother, "the Lord has told him to." On the contrary, hardly have we heard a word from him, when we react like a dog that has had a stone thrown at it: it leaves the person who threw the stone, and goes and bites the stone. That is what we do: we abandon God, who allows trials to come upon us to purify us from our sins; and we fall on our brother, saying, "Why did you do that to me?" And when we could draw much benefit from those sufferings, we fall into traps of our own devising, by not recognising that everything happens by God's providence, according to what is best for each person. May God give us understanding, through the prayers of the saints. Amen.

Other texts (taken from various Instructions and Letters of St Dorotheus)

9. (*Speaking of Adam*) When a man has no taste for self-accusation, he does not fear to accuse God himself.

(*Speaking of Adam and Eve*) But neither of the two stooped to accuse themselves, and neither of them showed the slightest humility.

10. (*Speaking of Adam and Eve*) Now you see clearly the state we have arrived at, and to what innumerable evils we have been brought by our passion for justifying ourselves, denying our fault; confidence in oneself and clinging to one's own will are the offshoots of pride, the enemy of God. By contrast, the ways of humility are accusing oneself, distrusting one's own judgement, and hatred of self-will, and these things enable our nature to be restored and purified through Christ's holy commandments.

91. Abba Zosimus was once asked to explain the saying, "where there is no irritation, there is no combat". He said that if, at the beginning of the quarrel, when the smoke and sparks begin to appear, one takes the initiative by accusing oneself and abasing oneself before the flame of anger is lit, then one remains at peace.

101. Every sin originates in the love of pleasure, or love of money, or vainglory. Lying, similarly, comes from one of these three passions. People lie either to avoid being accused and humiliated, or to satisfy a desire, or to achieve gain.

A liar's imagination is constantly at work, devising all possible subterfuges to attain his goal.

187. Fight to find a way of accusing yourself in everything, and hold fast to detachment towards knowledge.[4]

Believe that everything that happens to us, even the tiniest details, comes from God's providence, and you will bear whatever comes to you without impatience. Believe that contempt and insults are remedies for your soul's pride, and pray for those who mistreat you, considering them true doctors. Persuade yourself that anyone who hates humiliation hates humility, and that everyone who avoids unpleasant people, is avoiding sweetness.

Do not seek to know about the evil of your neighbour, and do not harbour suspicions against him. And if our malice does give birth to them, try and transform them into good thoughts.

196. Get it into your head that you have given pretext to temptation, even though at this moment you do not see why. Accuse yourself, have patience and pray, and I am confident that our Blessed Lord Christ will in his tenderness drive away the temptation.

30. In truth, nothing is more powerful than humility. Nothing is mightier than humility. If anything bad happens to the humble man, he immediately looks inside himself and judges that he deserves it. And he does not permit himself to reproach anyone or throw the blame on another. He simply bears it, without upset, without annoyance, and in all meekness. Therefore "humility is not irritated and does not irritate anyone." The Saint spoke truly: before anything else, we need humility.

63. Abba Poemen said that self-will is a steel wall between man and God. And, he added, "It is a stumbling-block", because it confronts God's will and sets up obstacles to it.

If a man renounces his own will, he can truly say, "with my God, I can scale any wall. As for God, his ways are perfect" (*Ps* 18[17]:30-31). What admirable words! Because when one has renounced one's own will, one travels the way of God without reproach. But if one obeys one's own will, one cannot see that God's way is perfect. If one receives a rebuke or a challenge, one turns away in contempt and rebels. How could one listen to another or follow their advice, if one is clinging to one's own will?

98. Never trust your suspicions, because a crooked measuring-rod makes even what is straight seem crooked. Suspicions are deceptive and harmful (this was a counsel from Abba John). Nothing is graver than suspicions. They are so harmful that in the long run they convince us and make us believe we have proof of certain things, which do not exist and have never existed.

97. A man who admits suspicions is a liar in his thought. If he sees two brothers talking, he thinks, "They are talking about me," and if they stop talking, then he thinks it is because he is present. If anyone says a word, he suspects it is to offend him. In short, in everything he suspects his neighbour and says, "It is because of me that he did this; it is because of me that he said that." Such is the man who

lies in his thought; he says nothing according to the truth, but all by conjecture. This is where indiscreet curiosity arises, and speaking badly of others, and the habit of going around listening, of arguing, and judging.

It happens, moreover, that someone fabricates suspicions, and then the facts show that they are true; and then, with the excuse of wanting to improve, the person goes around eavesdropping, telling himself, "When people speak against me, I will discover the fault that they see in me, and can correct myself." But from the start, this attitude originates in the Evil One. Because it is actually because of a lie that the person began to examine his conduct; in his ignorance he conjectured what he did not know. So how can a bad tree produce good fruit? If that person really wants to correct himself, he will not be upset when some brother tells him, "Don't do that," or "Why did you do that?" but will make him a profound reverence and thank him. Then he will improve. And if God sees that is his desire, he will not let such a person stray, but will certainly send him someone to correct him. But as for saying "It is for the sake of my own amendment that I believe my suspicions," and going around spying on others, taking note everywhere, all of that is a false excuse inspired by the devil, who wants to deceive us.

100. Let us learn never to believe our suspicions. There is nothing that is more conducive to neglecting our own sins,

because it leads us to occupy ourselves constantly with what does not concern us. Nothing good comes of that, but a thousand problems, a thousand sufferings, and we never acquire the peace that comes of the true fear of God. Therefore when our interior untruthfulness sows suspicions in us, let us change them on the spot into good thoughts, and then they will not harm us. For suspicions and suppositions are full of malice, and never leave our souls in peace. This is what is meant by being a liar in thought.

192. (*A letter to a brother who asked him about insensitivity of soul and the cooling-down of charity*)

Against insensitivity of soul, my brother, it is useful to read holy Scripture continually, as well as the "catanyctic sayings" [sayings that elicit compunction] of the godly Fathers, which invite one to think of the terrible judgements of God, to remember that the soul will leave the body and meet the terrible Powers against which it has committed evil in this short and miserable life; that it will also appear before the terrifying and incorruptible tribunal of Christ to render an account before God, his angels, and every creature: to render an account not only of actions but also words and thoughts. Remember constantly, too, these words that the terrible, just judge will say to those on his left: "Go away from me, with your curse upon you, to the eternal fire prepared for the devil and his angels" (*Mt* 25: 41). It is also good to remember the great human tribulations, because in that way also the hard and insensible soul melts, and becomes aware of its own unhappy state.

As for the weakening of fraternal charity, it comes from the fact that you consent to suspicious thoughts, and that you trust your own heart, and wish to suffer nothing against your will. In the first place, you should, with God's help, pay no attention to your suspicions, and rather apply yourself with all your strength to humbling yourself before your brethren, and denying your own will for their sakes. If one of them insults or injures you, pray for him, as the Fathers have said, considering that such behaviour will bring you great benefits and will cure you of the love of pleasure. If you follow that way, your anger will be calmed, since, according to the holy Fathers, charity "restrains anger". But above all pray to God to give you an alert and lucid spirit "to discover the will of God and know what is good, what it is that God wants, what is the perfect thing to do" (*Rm* 12:2), and the strength to be ready and quick to undertake every good work.

Sayings

17. It is impossible to be angry against one's neighbour unless one has first arisen against him in one's heart, and despised him, judging oneself superior to him.

18. If one is upset when one is corrected or accused concerning a passion, it is a sign that one has it voluntarily.

By contrast, receiving the accusation or correction peacefully shows that one is free from that passion, or that if one has it, it is not voluntary.

20. Since we are victims of our passions, we should never absolutely trust what our heart tells us, because a crooked measure makes what is straight crooked.

Endnotes

[1] Published in the *Boletín de Espiritualidad* of the Argentinian Province of the Society of Jesus, no. 87, May-June 1984.

[2] The devil does not only use lies to tempt us. A temptation may well be based on something true, but taken in a bad spirit. As Blessed Peter Faber taught: "I felt another desire in the Mass, to wit, that all the good that I might do, or think, or set in hand, etc., should be done in a good spirit, and not through means of a bad one. From there I went on to think how our Lord would not consider it good to reform some things in the Church after the manner of heretics; because, although they (like the devils) say many things that are true, they do not say them with the Spirit of Truth, which is the Holy Spirit" (*Memorial*, no. 51; cf. notes 84 and 375 of the Spanish edition, published by Ediciones Diego de Torres, San Miguel, 1983). Ideologies are largely built up on that basis. Although an ideology is apparently born of a truth, or at least of an opinion, in reality it is born of the will (or as Peter Faber puts it, of bad spirit). Hence an ideology should always be judged not on its content but on the underlying spirit, which is, precisely, not the spirit of truth.

[3] Cf. *The Way of Perfection*, Chapter 13.

[4] "Detachment (*apsephiston*) towards knowledge" is not easy to translate, because it contains a wealth of analysis and experience (cf. I. Hausherr, *Penthos*, p. 104). It could signify the total detachment that is manifested in the habit, or at least the resolve, not to want to give oneself, or accept from others, praise for any kind of superiority (cf. I. Hausherr, *Direction spirituelle en Orient autrefois*, p. 317).